ROCK | SALT | STONE

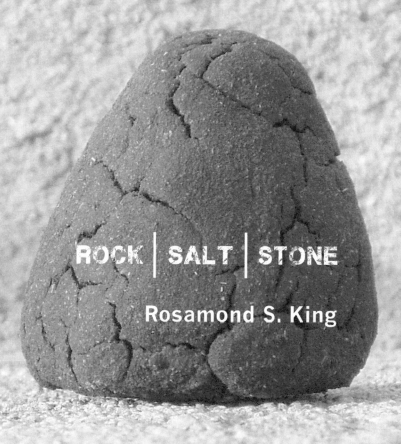

ROCK | SALT | STONE

Rosamond S. King

Nightboat Books
New York

© 2017 Rosamond S. King
All rights reserved
Printed in the United States

ISBN 978-1-937658-61-8   33614080800294

Design and typesetting by Margaret Tedesco
Text set in News Gothic and Adobe Caslon Pro

Cover/interior art by Rosamond S. King: *EROS*, 2010 (installation view). Henna mounds; dimensions variable. Full installation created in Partapur, Rajasthan, India.

Cataloging-in-publication data is available
from the Library of Congress

Distributed by University Press of New England
One Court Street
Lebanon, NH 03766
www.upne.com

Nightboat Books
New York
www.nightboat.org

To the people who taught me to take writing poetry for granted:
Halifax, Synthia, & Syneta King

For those told not to write, expected to suck salt,
left to die alone on a rock or under a stone.

ONE

    Bring Back   3

TWO

    [I was eating cereal and water]   15
    [the room gets/heavy]   16
    Lajablesse in Oakland   17
    Stranger in the Dark   21
    [Roll the curlers under.]   22
    [I cut off my feet]   23
    [need grows]   24
    [scrub dark and soiled areas.]   25
    for Isatou for Haddy for Adama for Elle   26
    [In the day/you strut]   28
    Tambourine   29
    bottle   30
    another day   31
    REPARATIONS   32

THREE

    [I cannot hula hoop anymore]   37
    [The family sound dry]   38
    In search of a word   39
    [There is no more reason]   42
    [each clump of grass or stone holds heat]   43
    first fever   44
    [The punctuation in between]   45
    Testing the Glass   46
    [you woke up yesterday and did not expect to die]   48

FOUR

    "She"   53
    Spit in a well   54
    [sex can, on occasion]   55
    [The slices of keratin that are her nails.]   56

[I fell in love with the market woman] 57

the pavement/road/stone glistens 58

Black girls taste like 59

you. nasty. 60

[I love myself/when] 61

Darling youuuuuuuuuuuuuuuuuuuuu zami 62

Experimints in Spellchick 66

we are all language poets 67

F IVE: SHADOW POEMS

the poem wet 71

The poem s t r e t c h e d out 72

the poem with overgrowth 73

the poem mud 74

the poem lyric 75

reaching 76

the poem blinged out 77

silent 78

SIX

[There are some caterpillars] 83

Sea Garden 84

[There is no heat in the hot.] 85

[I appreciate your work] 86

[Because evil] 88

(Name Withheld) 89

[Go home, water poet] 90

[memory is not true] 91

SEVEN

Old Head. 95

ABOUT THE BOOK 101

Notes and Additional Reading

Acknowledgements

ONE

Bring Back

My Eshu lies over the ocean
My Oshun lies inside the sea
Abiku cries down by the river
Don't bring back that body to me

Bring

Back

The douen is derived from abiku
And Oshun became Erzulie
My history lies under the overt
My heritage beyond the seen

My brawn it belongs to the Ogun
My blood it flows into the sea
The two meet inside a black body
And whisper *you fight to be free*

My bonnet flies along with Oshun
My bond it lies under the sea
A billion cries sent through my Eshu
Plea *bring bakra body to me*

The ancestors reached out to name me
There's Aku and Trini in me
They both can be traced to the same source
Of blood and of soil and sea

My Nyamo came over the ocean
My Oshun lives inside of me
With Eshu they're why I'm still living
This story flows into the sea

Bring

Back

TWO

I was eating cereal and water
when she came to buse me off
I made sure there were no crispies
in my teeth tightened my head tie
took up my voice and threw it at her

the room gets

                                        heavy

                                                          when she

folks start to feel weighed down

by her

the way she

they say
             her words are poison
                  taste like almonds
     they say her legs
       whips
               beating everything in sight

Lajablesse in Oakland

1

is who you tink
dat man tryin to film?

You seen it, it grainy-grainy
an far like a home porno.

He see a pretty dark skin gyul
in a long skinny skirt
twitchin she twitch
an he grin an he say
"tape rollin."
is only later
like he release from a spell
he realize a man was being beat
by police.
he never know
wha happn to de piece o tape
wit de piece o tail.

2

is not a cloven hoof
is a club foot.

Dat piece o ting
call heself a man
one night I holdin me face
an de fire in me head
come out through me mouth —
I cuss he slow, an when I finish
I say I gwine leave he.

He stan up watchin me
an when I finish he turn roun
an slash wit de machete.
Leave? He lean into me face.
Laughin. Leave now.

I had to bind me own foot.

He didn hardly come by after dat.
I suppose since I couldn get around to cook much or anyting else.

But when me foot heal, I go an stan up in de road where he mus pass
me comin back from de rumshop or whichever jamette he keepin
house wit now.

Is train tracks on de one side an forest on de odder an who runnin in
forest after dark.

I dress nice an pretty, an even wit de club foot I a prize because in dose
months me face done recover from takin licks. I want him to see I is
still a woman. A desirable woman. A woman who could still stan up. A
woman who was gwine to kill he. Only I ain thought too much bout
de killing part. I ain bring no machete, not even a big stick or skillet.
But den all thinkin was to stop because I see he.

An as he get closer an he know it me I start walkin. Not good because
I not too use to de club foot yet. An I smile, for I know if ever will
could do anyting, my will gwine to kill dis man. An I limpin an he lips
begin to tremble like fryin pork an

Lord how he frighten!

An I limpin an is de forest to one side, de train tracks on de odder an
me dead center wit death on my mind. Suddenly so he freeze turn an
leap. Tryin to jump de freight! It go so fast, I not really sure wha happn.
But as he catch up on a car an look home free one minute, de nex he
dangling by a foot, screamin like a goat bein killed slowly.

How de conductor didn hear me don know, because everyone in de
parish dat night wonderin wha obeah ting cause a goat neck to be
slit so slow dat it scream so long. But he soon stop an as people piece
togedder de body dey piece togedder a story of wha happn.

I limp up to de rum shop an walk in among all dose men, some o dem
no better dan de one mash up by de train tracks, an their silence hol
me up. I down six shot o rum — Hubert never ask for payment yet —
an walk out straight same way. From dat night, no man speak to me.

They call me lajablesse. Devil woman. De woman dem too bad talk
me in de street. But when night fall dey come try maco me wit sweet
tamarind an cloth no one will sell me in de store. Bless, dey say, for den
dey say I am blessed, Bless dis man does treat me bad, bad. You cyan do
him someting for me — ?

What I gwine say? Me ain have no money, dey treat me like I is kill
priest in town, I say I go see wha I could do. Is allyou own fear an
longin an hate dat is give me power. Is allyou make me a real lajablesse.

You know, is really Sou who bind
me foot. I couldn have done it.
I shame to say it, but I was scared o she —
you know what they say. But dark
as it was I see she had no wings, an her
skin was intact an dark as mine.

3

Of course I had to leave dat town. Anywhere I go now I only passin through — an I don see Sou for a long time. Is so how I reach Oakland, for I find dat men does do evil all over, an since I could travel I could see bout evil anywhere. You know I ain have but one power. Dat is de power to make man see himself. Dat sweetman mashup on de train tracks — is not me who kill him! He reach up on de train an as he turn to laugh in me face, he see himself. An what he see so ugly, it frighten him so, he lose his grip an baps! all finish.

An de man in Oakland. He not a good man, mind, he not good atall. But he don deserve beatin in de street like a dog. An when I see de cokey-eye man wit a video, me tink TECHNOLOGY. Now dere is a way to get a whole heap a people to see demselves. An it could use to get retribution in dis world as well as sen some folks into de nex. I not anybody special. I is just your retribution.

So I go all over. An I always lookin fine, because men an women always tryin to sweet me up, tryin to see wha dey could get from me, wha dey could get me to do. An de more dey look at me, de more dey see demself.

Is one other power I have. Let's call it de Still Here power. De here change an change an change again, but I still here.

An dat is all I really want to say, dat
I not dead yet.

Stranger in the Dark

Eyes slithering down
chest eyes seizing
neck eyes spying
legs looks saying
not woman but
fe-male meaning
one who can be fucked.

Roll the curlers under.
Keep them close to the scalp.
Curlicue, curly yew. Scalped.
Close to and don't brush, just run
your fingers through.

I cut off my feet
put them in a pan
of olive oil the better
to make them soft.
I singed my hair all
over with the iron.
I sprayed acid in my
eyes to make them
more mysterious.
I rinsed my mouth
with bleach to make
my teeth more white.
I bound myself with
steel inventing a
perfect curved figure.
You think you're
going to leave me?

need grows

as negroes

come & go

scrub dark and soiled areas. scrub clean, scrub glee. pat dry.

sterility guaranteed if package has been opened or tampered (tampon, tamper away!). otherwise all openings orifices are productive and procreative.

child safe droppers, usually on the head. height and impact surface vary, though velocity is constant (provide velocity equation, using gravity).

our thick, elegant, nongreasy formulation will be absorbed by poors. you'll never have to wash again.

for Isatou for Haddy for Adama for Elle

someone came looking for your kind and you looked at her
considered how much she is not from here
Asia all over her face and hair
her English worse than yours

and you opened your mouth

whispering in your own compound
            afraid still
but fear is as common as your own hair
    you wash it and comb it and
            plait it in rows

I am looking for you
    I am looking for our kind
will you open your mouth to me?
  we can scratch and oil each
   other's scalp
      if we only open our mouths
if we plait and unplait each
            other's heads
    we don't even have to speak

        it may never
      happen
you and I are dangerous
        to each other
   one whisper causes bush fire here —
you and I
      may even be cousins

if we never meet
if we never get to whisper together
it is enough that
   you opened your mouth
it is enough
   knowing
 that you exist

      my other
   in the long hours of doing
      and undoing your hair
listen to the whispers
   you will know
   it is me
 you will recognize
your own silent scream

In the day
you strut.

Night fear is your skin
membrane flexing over
muscles and fascia. This is
how you live, so much so that you forget
until someone
reminds you
you have too much flesh
in too many places. until
you realize you're looking for danger and escapes
judging other pedestrians' threat.
Your skin, you live it till the light

Tambourine

(when you hit it, it makes noise)

My little tambourine my
darling baby boy I beat you so
I know you're real. My tambourine.
Where would I be if you didn't
cry and heave? I scratch your
skin because I can't believe
there's bone under your soft
soft flesh. I hit you and you
ring. My little tambourine.

bottle holds milk bottle
   like a breast oblong
bottle give bottle to baby
   baby suck bottle baby drink
milk from bottle like a breast
   baby suck bottle oblong
bottle holds milk

another day

sometimes you just get tired
carrying all the things in your hands
all the people on your back and
you stumble
keep going
you cannot fall you
cannot   cannot
                        fall
think of the people
men and women who thought your back was strong
cutting their feet on the earth's stones
babies rolling into the mud

REPARATIONS

see   through   people!
                                        on sale today!
35 year old   boys   and girls
breeding boys
                    to lighten your race
breeding girls
                    for fun and profit
backs bent every morning
legs open every night
see   through   people!
                              cheap!

THREE

I cannot hula hoop any more
I am told my heart is rock
stone jewel and shiny lizards
for intestines but it's true
I can't hula hoop any more
not now with melons
in my chest and breadfruit
at the bottom of my back
with leaves and branches
of the flamboyant broadening
from my head boiled indigo
bluing my lips

The family sound dry
— not the looks, the voice.
Bizarre secondary attributes
physical similarities
that come and go. She
a sister mom aunt spook
someone with a tenor and tone
exactly like her dad's. She'll
go on in fits and starts.
They belong
to a weird kind. Someone
wants to ask, wonders
about their family's hair
and hands, if after death
they stop, or go on forever.

In search of a word

Benn
Ñaar
Ñett
Ñeent
Juroom
Juroom benn

when you have language but no one
to speak it with
eventually the words
fall on the ground
unremembered

Juroom ñaar
Juroom ñett
Juroom ñeent
Fukk
Fukk ak benn
Right?
And now this is all:
Nanga def hello, how are you?
and then hands up
stopping code
switching *I don't know*
anymore degg olof tutti rek
Fukk ak ñaar
Fukk ak ñett
Fukk ak ñeent
Fukk ak juroom
Fukk ak juroom benn
I will not ask you to count

what got left behind.
Do you remember December?
When home was snow surrounding fireplace
almost all your children together and
cozy it was cozy –?
Fukk ak juroom ñaar
Fukk ak juroom ñett
Fukk ak juroom ñeent
Ñaar fukk
My well-rehearsed speech, the book
about parenting such a child, the phone
number for PFLAG, the passage
from a novel, a mother telling a daughter she knows
without saying she knows
Ñaar fukk ak benn
Ñaar fukk ak ñaar
Ñaar fukk ak ñett
Ñaar fukk ak ñeent

Lesbian was only said once, but love
three or four times. Do you remember
December? Maybe should have
waited for summer, daylight
at least, so it wouldn't all
seem so foreign. *This was one*
of the things of this country
from which we were trying
to save you. Yes
your grammar
was perfect.

Ñaar fukk ak juroom
There is not

even a word in
our language
for this.

Ñaar fukk ak juroom benn
Do you want this sentence back?
I give it to you now clean, polished
from years of repetition. Without
malice — just it is yours and
I don't want it anymore.
Ñett fukk
There are words for this
in our language.
doom ju jigéen
Yaay Mama
doom ju góor
Papa Baay
Sissy
Auntie
Cousin
Uncle
Ñaar fukk ak juroom ñett
Oumar
Benjamin
Juroom ñeent fukk ak juroom ñeent
Rosamond
Olufunke
Teemeer ak benn
In our language there are words for
nob
bëgg
love

There is no more reason
water to your face
The sea is there, and during
season you cannot ask
water or salt.

The mother said. How
know? The daughter
you fed me with
blood. I know.

to bring
the daughter said
the rainy
for more

do you
smiling:
your

each clump of grass or stone holds heat
(like) every imprint of my wide foot
smiling broadly at no one
look up; look up the view
from there is vast
and you do not know more than any stone.

very clean is the slate of your face
not smirking, your face not mean
this is my favorite; a photograph of water
propped on pillows before me
what were you thinking, you

"there is no cure"

first fever
whole air baking you
      water making steam with skin
            then mud snakes
   pain starts (behind intestines
     you in a small room
forehead against cool wall
   all this before blood
     coming in two days time
  groping for ibuprofen
always your mouth closed
  pain a small animal
chewing a perimeter in your flesh
  because those whose ears can hear
this telling this woman's thing
    make their eyes small
      are you creating demons
  or maybe just writing poems
always your mouth closed
  sinking you deflated
    even then no sounds
just the inside flesh

The punctuation in between
the fact that you manage to function
twisted necessity to proof
of deception, wasting every one's time
as if buildings all in white are amusement
parks; strangers' hands on your body the ferris wheel
cold hard silver between your legs cotton candy

Testing the Glass

No one within thousands of miles to hold her hand and even then, well. It should be four-something by now, she looks onto the street to see if the earth has heaved up clods of dirt and mulch, like her body erupts with things that do not belong there, like her body attacking and running away at the same time. How do you fight that? She tests the glass. How much pressure, velocity would it take for her hand to splinter it, go through? And the screen — would it be easier or more resistant — ? But she lives alone, so who would clean up the glass, pick shards from her knuckles, keep the wind from snaking in? So she looks at the tree, directly in front of the building, leaning from the time she moved in. If it fell now, it would destroy two cars and tear a hole in the sidewalk. Not knowing what to pray for, she wills the tree to lean some more, regresses to a childhood wish for telekinesis, not to turn out the light without leaving warm covers, but to force the earth — since people are no use — to destroy something, to evidence, to point and say there is anguish here! All she has is some blankness and a pen. The pen fails her, even, and it's five something now, the heat kicked back on, papers delivered and no broken glass and no heaving earth and a pen that scratch, scratch, refuses to write. So she walks — she can do that — gets another, imagines the pages stained with her own fluids. And after all, she could be dead already. What's a few unidentified masses, inconclusive tests, a chronic disease or two?

What is a future of injections and surgery and medication? She lives in a country where she can get them, and has insurance, for now, so who really cares if there's no one to lean on? At least now, while she's standing. Besides. The glass is whole, probably thicker than she thinks, and behind it the strung steel of the screen, and beyond that the tree leaning still. They will know when to fall apart, when to collapse. If her body cleaves from itself or implodes, she will not be betrayed by people and the whole earth and a pane of glass and steel. Or by a pen. They will know when to upheave, they will hold her hand and say, see this destruction? Look at it, it's up there, in apartment three a. She can last until then. She can wait.

you woke up yesterday and did not expect to die
so of course the night seemed different, smiling.
before sleeping you sighed, and then
and then, and then? Tomorrow you will
look in a glass and nearly trip
startled by your own beauty,
outlined by the sun.

FOUR

"She"

sees
a girl, pants snug and low
baseball shirt slid into boxers
watches
the woman swagger by
wants
a stick, a dick
has
this white dress, part 1942 fits
close and just below the knee
part 2018, cotton and lycra
licking coca cola shape
dreams
daily, of being
in this dress walking
to a woman like that
and leaning in
close, so she can smell cologne and
pomade, right up
on her
so she can feel the dick stick
wants but does not dare
watches
woman swagger away
blinks
swings
coca cola shape

Spit in a well
turn 6 times to the left
she will fall down with
belly pain and not see relief
till she calls your name

sex can, on occasion, be replaced with salt. white corn tortilla chips, for instance. or popcorn that is not overcome with butter. when only a few pieces are tasted the tart and tang will arouse. salt is heat; it produces the wet and contractions of swallowing. it causes the tongue to swell. occasionally, sometimes hours later you will discover a grain on your lip. the sensation of hardness melting to hot will press the lips together and bring you back again.

The slices of keratin that are her nails. The extended digits writing gestures on air when she speaks. Her earth hair. The depression of her ear and the interrupting bulge of her knee. Let me let me with her unattractive feet. Her used feet and the web of skin between the first finger and the finger that is not one. Her left nipple that pouts which I have not yet seen by fluorescent light —

I fell in love with the market woman
when I was supposed to be feeling tomatoes
I smelled the green pepper sweat of her flesh
leaning into the christophine I searched
for the salt fish scent in her lap.
As I waited fingers weighed me, fingers dropped me
together in pieces — rough, but not too
rough. I reach out with the money and I'm
vortexed into her young-old, old-young
eyes thinking, today she will pull me into
her narrows that widen and widen, but she just says
"go long gyal."

the pavement/road/stone glistens.
sight is not
touch — it looks
wet and slick
but is only wet.
I had a woman like
that, we used
baby oil and spit.
The mirage road
beckons-slide on
me, skate, lay in
the sparkling sun,
dip a finger and suck

Black girls taste like

those hard bits of brown
sugar you roll with
your tongue
and   you're rolling it
and swallowing the sweet
and before you know it
it's gone

Black girls taste like
those hard bits of sugar
and something deep fried.

you. nasty. you
wanna hear my voice. you
heaving on top o me. you
n your wet tongue in
sundry places. tasting. you
cussin under
your breath. in my mouth. you
pleading for more from me n you
pushing right up to the point of pain.
you askin me questions when I
can't think straight. you with your
hand digging past exhaustion
coming up with desire and desire.
you. smirk-faced girl in the mirror.
you nasty.

(I love myself when I am laughing, and then again when
I am looking mean and impressive. — Zora Neale Hurston)

I love myself
  when I am

      he hee! ha ha ha whoooeeee!

You didn't think
  I could do it   didja?
    Thought I was hard
      like stone like rock
        candy   *mean*
          and then again   *mean*
      thought you could melt

Watch out man be
          cause
  I   love myself
  I love   myself
  I love myself when I am
    andthenagain
  I love myself
        when I am looking

Darling youuuuuuuuuuuuuuuuuuuu zami

Mammy	Zami	Auntie	Nanny
(Ain't she ?)			
les amies	*lesamies*	*lezamis*	lezzies

■ ■

funny. maco. macoman. macomère.
mek yu come. mek yu mudder come.

(metrosexual androgynous lesbian chic

steuuuppppsssssss

flirting, flirting…
— cute'll kill ya

you got a mouth full of fuck you
and a cunt full of fuck me

■ ■

Query
Query Nation
Query: woman-(open category)-loving
        woman-(culturally-loaded signifier)-sexing-woman (

Query: Nation (with definable borders crossable with expired
passports)

Query: nation?

····································

(he always wanted to
stick his finger
in a dyke)

dick dyke deck   edge
deckled dimpled   edges
dumped rumpled   edgy   edged

make your mouth a Sakia Gunn
I'm not interested I'm a
     butch trans genderfuck aggressive queer inthelife

he always wanted
to stick his
····································

If you talk out
the side of your neck
the soucouyant will fuck you dry

····································

Triage.
Mareeage,
Miscarreeage of just this assimilation

crouch in the streets
gem in the sheets

One of the Children
went In the Life
Came Out with We. Are. Family!
get used
to it

laddies & gentle dykes
the state of the civil union is

strongarming

Bi the trans
figuration
questioning whose spirit
trance fender care
inter ex
day thespians
aren't you overcome?

■ ■

so dem may
sodomite

■ ■

if you talk out the side

if you   talk

if you

darling youuuuuuuuuuu zami
honest you do
honest you do
honest you do
(woooooooaaaa-ahhhhhhh!)

Experimints in Spellchick

If you interrogate what hippens in the psat, you well bee able to predick the futour. Her genus lies in the fat that her writing perfectually invects the reeder in. [sic! dangling preparation]
Are you cop-dependent? Take these supple testes and keep track of your scare. It is rediculous to right this as prose. But the assay is paid more than the verso.

If it
snot a prose
poom is
it less
xprinti-mental
avent guard
in no votive end
market able?
Dint be two heard on the yolks in charge. They ear gist weeping the fits of their Labradors.

we are all
language poets
just some of us more
than others
we are all language
poets just
some of us more
than others

we are all language
poets
just
some of us are
others

we are all language
poets just
some of us

we are all   we are all
language   language
poets   poets
just   just
some of us   some of us
                                    others

                                                        we are all
                                                        language
                        poets

                                                        just
                                                        some of us
            others

FIVE

Shadow Poems

the poem wet

sssssssss
me hair on yu cheek   *den*
me hair on yu belly
an yu still want more?
sssssssssst!
you yes you yes
where there is no rest we rest
— the blood never stops
you yes
there is no outside
feel this, here

The poem s t r e t c h e d out

Body sigh
Body shhhhhhhhhhhhhh
sssssssssssssssss
     follicles and epithelial cells
gastronomy and desire
ssssssssss
Body mine
Without or in the absence of
rest or repose on the divan I always
   wanted with the women I've always wanted
Body
Mine!
Body blood
white and red
   blood acid fluid wetness
     mine
Me in the absence of without
external
alone, still
Touch, feel skin and under that —

the poem with overgrowth

enticing flesh covered mandible shsh
full not sated the appearance hhhhh
of the other both shocks and sssssssss
awesome ssshhsssssshhhhhhhhhhssssh
sssshsssssssshhhhhhsshhhsshshhhsssshh

in the absence of time without end h
without peace liquid bodies perpetually
you know
the presence growing stalks in sssssssss
your fingers and feet hshshsshshs

the poem mud

goooooood
gone
your grit
glistens
**

gather gristle
for my greedy gall
girly guy-girl
getting
gutted I guess
guilty jilted
jist
guessed again

the poem lyric

shshssshshhh
(insert yourself here)
(your cheek and hair)
(sour desirous indecision)
(your lack of sleep
your beating blood)

reaching

you
no
me
no
us
yes
we
then
who
with
you
not
me
in the absence of me you
all ready cook, but de food na nuff
in the absence of us me
de rain a fall but de dutty tuff
re think
who are you to say
absolutely
if no yes I alone craving
belly
food
rockstone
ground
yours
truly, rain
giving
blood

the poem blinged out

Flash! Shine!

(Me. Belly. Full. But. Ah. Hungry!)
    tattooed lips and twirled-up hair
  This is me in Lagerfeld. This is me in
    Versace.
(And we'll keep. Goin. Till six in de. Mornin.)
    flash! shine.
Blood is for veins, asphalt
  metal and leather
 This is me

                  (flash)

 This is me in

                  (shine)

silent

```
 .  .  .
 *  *  *

 ~  ~  ~
→↑↓
 /  /  /

 .  ,  .
 ↑↓
Ø*Ø.~
```

SIX

There are some caterpillars whose state of being is not a preface to winged existence.

These caterpillars always cling to a surface, and will not exchange leaves for pollen.

Sea Garden
Dead man's fingers —
short and still
or waving spindles
brain coral,
mountain coral
ground small — they
would be pebbles
if they weren't shards
hiding places
for trumpet
fish and crabs
live and dead coral
What is sand made of?
Who is to know
which is coral
and which
is bone
From the surface you
can see dark
patches where sea grass
and spirit hair grow

There is no heat in the hot.
It ran for
a long time, but was
only lukewarm.

I appreciate your work

but gristle should be turned into flesh?

I like the body will remember. But what if the body isn't?

started with the feet.
didn't tickle with you.

learned have knots at bottom of shoulders, just behind armpits.
learned piece of muscle in left calf directly connected to clit. learned
back is hard.

But you knew that already.

left face impassive
when made me angry decided
wouldn't give
any response at all.

made you angry took it out on me.

moaned once but didn't realize it.

touched my butt weren't supposed to. straddled me
both knew weren't supposed to.

Anybody hearing grunts would have thought.

played with my hair too long. said something about it in your

language to other

girl said something about it back.

worst part was touched my face. never give you face — or scalp.

back was very hard. didn't find.

didn't like facing up, closed eyes. sure you smiling.

can't really remember face.

worst part was fingers. hanging limp hands. wanted
them. got really, really cold.

Before and after dressed. <u>thank you</u> in your language.

didn't know didn't see you turned away.

Afterwards scrubbed for long time. trying to clean and dirty.

did not think of at all.

don't look different, even with clothes off. don't feel different. Really. do walk a little, but not even notice that.

shooting in the next room. only pretending.

flossed even though twice already. wanted to be completely clean, after.

different if we spoke the same language? less pure?

worked really hard. noticed when paused for breath. tried to breathe with you.

used fists, elbows, heels — climbed on top of needed leverage.

straddled. even though knew weren't supposed to.

maybe wanted to see if could leave marks. if color would separate from skin.

mostly remember not recalling face.

didn't send this. remember where met, but don't speak the same language.

Because evil

Because
         e   tr
      v   y   a
       i   l   v
         l n   el
    can o
                    i
                      n
                         a
    t h g i a r t s
          l
           i
         n
          e

(Name Withheld)

according to an official source,
according to [name withheld], a research company,
according to someone who spoke on the condition of anonymity,
according to a source close to the president,
according to friends and acquaintances who have known the accused
    a long time,
according to a woman who did not wish to reveal her name,
according to a man who identified himself only as "Stumpy,"
according to documents obtained by this pocm,
according to unidentified sources quoted in other media,
according to leading analysts,
according to industry experts,
according to a company executive,
according to industry insiders,
according to campaign staffers,
according to someone in a position to know,

Go home, water-poet

Into traveling machines, your feet

Into movement

Wetness

You will always sink in tar and blood

Go home, poet

To water.

memory is not true
but thread raveled
or unraveled, embroidered
or slack.

thread itself won't
usually
kill, but can strangle.

more often it reminds
or leads, is added
to mend or is
fingered and fingered
until the straight
line comes away

SEVEN

Old Head.

Old Head.

You remember Old Head. The woman in the small house? She was Ugly. Face filled with pits and valleys so you didn't know where her nose was. She was Fat. Couldn't tell her from coral or stone. Like the one they used to roll in front of Our Lord's tomb. Now, you remember. You know what happened to Old Head? I think she started off like anyone else. Eating and washing and saying hello. But she outlasted the people who remembered how she came to live near us, in the small house in the back of the road. People stopped being kind. People whispered as she passed. Stopped returning her greetings. Then they said things to her in the street. Then they shouted them. Their children learned how to do this, and to peep in her windows. They thought she was strange and otherwordly. Didn't you? I think she started off like anyone else. Going out and coming back in the daylight. And saying hello. But when the people removed her place with us. Well. I think she allowed herself to become strange. She made herself otherworldly. And then I think she began to hate herself too. Woke up in bed and stayed there. For days, I mean she stayed there. She lay there, one hand holding the other, until she willed herself into two different people. The one who hated herself like other people did. And the one who didn't know who this person they created was. That's what I think she did. A child peeping in saw her. Laying there, one hand holding the other.

when he realized that he and this woman whose hand was on top of
his had come from the Old Head. well. he rolled over and fucked her.
put his hand over her mouth as her eyes opened. when he was finished
went out looking for a peach. she watched him go and then wondered
why she was alone. washed her legs, face, mouth. looked at this small
house which was old. wondered who lived there. did she live there?
she must. her mind was the sea, returning to the same places with no
knowledge of having been there before. when the man came back he
was rolling a pit in his mouth. spat it down. watched the pale dust
rise and settle. went into the small house. looked at the woman, who
showed no more resemblance to the Old Head than he. this woman
whose face was blank as a stone. didn't look like anybody. didn't seem
to recognize him. didn't object to him either. he beat her for not
knowing. he beat her for being blank. he beat her to beat the blankness
out of her. and always a hand over her mouth or an arm necklacing her
throat. after his own personal eruption, a pulling on of pants. going out
to look for fruit. and so. for him each day was a reminder of the days
before. and the days before reminded him of the first day he opened
his eyes a man. knowing where he came from. hating his genesis.
hating the knowledge of it. hating her. for her each day was a first day.
wondering who was her mind and body. silently introducing herself to
ground, sky, water, small house. not questioning a man who seemed to
know already. his hand stopped going over her mouth. he believed she
could not scream either.

on this day she was washing. saw a rainbow on her thigh. turned.
there was a dark whirlpool on her shoulder. a sun setting on her eye.
slowly she bent. stopped. turned. arched. all of the world on her body.
he stepped home. spat the stone of a plum. it rolled, dusted with dirt,
stopped. she heard this and then silence. he pushed the door. she stood.
her head began tilting to the right. saw this man. who her mind. like
the sea. with no memory. did not know. but her body. her body with
the world pressed into it. knew. he watched her. strange today. standing
nude. like a rubbing stone where his hands, elbows, feet had used her.
her body knew. she screamed and there was sound. a great cleaving.
her body knew. rushed at him. this man. beat her world into his body.
him on the ground. when he realized. raised his hands. her body found
something. brought it down hard. after. she walked to the sea. took
note of where her feet were. sat in the sand and watched herself. her
body learned her. each whirlpool and sunset and rainbow. said this has
been done to me. floated on herself on water. cleaned herself with salt
and aloe. returned to the small house. by putting her feet in the same
places. stepped over the man. thinking. I have done this. I have been
here. learned the word before. looked. turned around. was gone.

ABOUT THE BOOK

everything I write is true; everything I write is a lie

Notes and Additional Reading

I have three places: The Gambia, Trinidad and Tobago, and Brooklyn, New York; most of these poems were written in these places. Some of these poems were written in other places, including Shanghai.

General Additional Reading
Anything by Kamau Brathwaite, Jayne Cortez, Edna St. Vincent Millay, Harryette Mullen, and M. NourbeSe Philip. *Cote ci Cote la: Trinidad and Tobago Dictionary* by John Mendes.

Bring Back

Eshu, Oshun, and Ogun are deities from the Yoruba religion that are also found in syncretic religions in the Caribbean, especially Trinidad and Tobago, Cuba, Haiti, and their diasporas. Erzulie is a Vodoun deity or lwa.

Bakra is slang for a white person in many English-speaking Caribbean countries. Some say it comes from the phrase "back raw."

Among the Yoruba, abiku are children who die before puberty and are believed to deliberately and repeatedly die and be born again. Similarly, the douen of Trinidad are the spirits of children who die before being baptized, who cause mischief, especially luring living children into the forest.

The Aku are an ethnic group in The Gambia and Sierra Leone. Trini is short for Trinidadian.

Nyamo is a Mandinka word that means spiritual strength or power. *Additional Reading: Creole Religions of the Caribbean: An Introduction from Vodou and Santeria to Obeah and Espiritismo*, by Margarite Fernandez Olmos & Lizabeth Paravisini-Gebert; "The Concept of Abiku" by Timothy Mobolade in *African Arts* Vol. 7, No. 1 (Autumn, 1973).

Lajablesse in Oakland

Lajablesse (from la diablesse, French for female devil) is a folk character found in Trinidad and Tobago and other places in the Caribbean. She is a beautiful woman who wears a long dress to hide the fact that one of her feet is in fact a cloven hoof. The lajablesse is said to seduce men and then kill them. "Sou" is short for soucouyant, another Caribbean folk character, an old woman who at night is said to shed her skin, become a ball of fire, and suck the blood or life spirit out of children.

In search of a word

All of the non-English words in "In search of a word" are Wolof. This poem was featured in a short video of the same name created and directed by Alison Duke.

PFLAG is Parents and Friends of Lesbians and Gays (www.pflag.org).

Several of the poems in **Section Three** are part of the "endo poems" series, which explores living with chronic pain and chronic illness (such as endometriosis), the pathologization of women's bodies, and the challenges of navigating the medical industry.

Additional Reading: The Endo Patient's Survival Guide: A Patient's Guide to Endometriosis & Chronic Pelvic Pain by Andrew S. Cook and Libby Hopton; *The Doctor Will See You Now: Recognizing and Treating Endometriosis* by Tamer Seckin.

[I fell in love with the market woman] was originally written for Patricia Powell.

Darling youuuuuuuuuuuuuuuuuuuuuuu zami

Additional Reading: Zami: A New Spelling of My Name by Audre Lorde; *Island Bodies: Transgressive Sexualities in the Caribbean Imagination* by Rosamond S. King.

Shadow Poems

These poems are part of a larger series, the result of a game I created, inspired by poet Erica Hunt's exercise to mirror a partner and then "break" the mirror.

Take any poem you have written and rewrite it. The next day, rewrite the poem you wrote the day before, and so on. You can either consecutively write different shadows of a single poem, or each poem can be the shadow of the one before it.

[Because evil] was inspired by a Chinese saying.

Acknowledgments

A core group of other artists and writers have challenged and encouraged my poetry for more than twenty years — the friendship and creative comradeship of Gabrielle Civil, Madhu Kaza, Swati Khurana, and Zetta Elliott continues to be both sustaining and invaluable.

Another core group has consistently supported and "shown up" for me and for my creative work: deep thanks for the fellowship of Olu George, Andrea Morton, and Nadine Rogers.

Duriel E. Harris is the metaphorical midwife of *Rock | Salt | Stone* and the book is all the better for it.

Many individuals made interventions that specifically encouraged the publication of this book; they include Purvi Shah, Evie Shockley, Gina Athena Ulysse, and Paolo Javier.

Poets House, Dixon Place, and Belladonna* have been longtime supporters, curating me into readings and programs, and providing hours of inspiration through their thoughtful presentation of other poets' work.

Several poems in this book first appeared (often in earlier versions) in the pages of journals and anthologies staffed by unpaid, overworked seraphim. My thanks to the editors of: *Harriet* (the Poetry Foundation blog); *Tuesday; The Black Scholar* (rest in peace, Robert Chrisman); *Body of Words: Performance Texts*, a Belladonna* Chaplet; *Caribbean*

Erotic; Surviving in the Hour of Darkness: The Health & Wellness of Women of Colour and Indigenous Women; MaComère; Beyond the Frontier: African American Poetry for the 21st Century; Downtown Brooklyn; Onionhead; and *Kindergarde: Experimental Poems for Children.* Thanks also to the residencies I have participated in at Alice Yard, Norcroft, and the Virginia Center for Creative Arts, and to the curators who programmed me into dozens of readings and performances in Africa, the Caribbean, and the USA.

Jen Bervin was an incredible mentor when I was a Poets House Fellow — flowers of handmade paper at her feet! Thanks also to the other Poets House Fellows, who created a fun and supportive space to emerge from the "emerging" category — and thanks to Cornelius Eady and Jean Valentine, who gave thoughtful comments on my work through that program. I am also fortunate to have learned from formal workshops with Kenneth A. McClane and Erica Hunt.

Finally, my deep thanks to the dedicated Nightboat team — publisher Stephen Motika and managing editor Lindsey Boldt — and to the Council of Literary Magazines and Presses who provided support, via the Jerome Foundation, to get this book to as many readers as possible.

Jayne Cortez. Jayne Cortez. Jayne Cortez. She taught me that poetry is work, that poets should be paid, and that the necessary work of poetry does not replace other necessary work in the world. She will rest in peace when there is justice; until then, we are fortunate her work will continue to protest and laugh on our behalf.

¡ laurie pea : squeak, k'bao. mwah !

Rosamond S. King is a creative and critical writer, performer, and artist whose work is deeply informed by the many cultures and communities she is part of, by history, and by a sense of play. Her poetry has been published in more than two dozen journals and anthologies, and she has performed in theatres, museums, nightclubs, and traditional literary venues in Africa, the Caribbean, Europe, and throughout North America. She has also received numerous honors, including a Fulbright Award and fellowships from the Woodrow Wilson, Mellon and Ford Foundations, Poets House and the Franklin Furnace Fund. She is the author of the chapbook, *At My Belly and My Back* and the critical book, *Island Bodies: Transgressive Sexualities in the Caribbean Imagination*, which won the 2015 Caribbean Studies Association Gordon K. and Sybil Lewis Prize for the best book in Caribbean studies.

King holds a Ph.D. in Comparative Literature with a minor in Performance Studies from New York University, and is an Associate Professor in the English Department at Brooklyn College, part of the City University of New York. The goal of her work is to make people feel, wonder, and think, in that order.

Photo by Iryna Fedorovska.